AI for Smart Pre-Teens and Teens Ages 10-19:
Using Artificial Intelligence to Learn, Think, and Create

© 2023 by Dr. Leo Lexicon

Notice of Rights

All rights reserved. No portion of this publication may be reproduced, distributed, or transmitted in any form or by any means, electronic or mechanical, including photocopying, recording, or any information storage and retrieval system, without prior written permission from the author. Reproduction or translation of this work in any form beyond that permitted by Sections 107 or 108 of the 1976 United States Copyright Act is strictly prohibited. No companion books, summaries, or study guides are authorized under this notice. For other permission requests, please contact the author.

Liability Disclaimer

The information provided within this book is for general informational purposes only. While every effort has been made to keep the information up-to-date and correct, there are no representations or warranties, express or implied, about the completeness, accuracy, reliability, suitability, or availability with respect to the information, products, services, or related graphics contained in this book for any purpose. Any use of this information is at your own risk.

This book may contain affiliate links. It is important to note that the author only recommends products or services that they genuinely believe will be beneficial to the reader. In order to ensure trust and transparency, this disclosure complies with the rules set by the Federal Trade Commission. The support received through these affiliate links helps sustain the creation of valuable content. We appreciate the understanding and support of all readers.

The author, company, and publisher shall in no event be held liable for any loss or other damages, including but not limited to special, incidental, consequential, or other damages. This disclaimer applies to any damages caused by any failure of performance, error, omission, interruption, deletion, delay in transmission or transmission, defect, computer malware, communication line failure, theft, destruction, or unauthorized access to or use of records, whether for breach of contract, tort, negligence, or under any other cause of action. By reading this book, you agree to use the contents entirely at your own risk and that you are solely responsible for your use of the contents. The author, company, and publisher do not warrant the performance or applicability of any references listed in this book. All references and links are for informational purposes only and are not warranted for content, accuracy, or any other implied or explicit purpose.

AI for Smart

Pre-Teens and Teens Ages 10-19

Using Artificial Intelligence to Learn, Think, and Create

by

Dr. Leo Lexicon

AI for Smart

Pre-Teens and Teens Ages 10-19

Using Artificial Intelligence to Learn, Think, and Create

"AI for Smart Kids" takes you on an exciting trip into the world of AI. This interesting and educational book will show you the wonders of AI in a way that is both fun and easy to understand.

Discover how AI is changing almost every aspect of our lives, and how it will become a feature of our future. You will learn about the interesting history of AI, from the first ideas about it in ancient times to the amazing innovations that led to its birth in the 1950s. Follow along as AI develops and becomes a part of our daily lives, changing education, jobs, creativity, and even healthcare in big ways.

You will be amazed at how AI works by learning about things like data, machine learning, code, computer vision, and natural language processing. Don't worry about the technical terms, they will be explained to you in ways you can easily understand them.

The book also talks about how important ethical AI is and what risks it might bring. We all need to think about how we can use AI in a responsible way. This book tells you about what to look for and where to look, and it provides useful resources for you to learn more, solve puzzles, and learn how to code.

Dr. Leo Lexicon is an educator and author. He is the founder of Lexicon Labs, a publishing imprint that is focused on creating entertaining books for active minds.

CONTENTS

CHAPTER 1 1

INTRODUCTION 1
    WELCOME TO THE WORLD OF AI 1

CHAPTER 2 4

WHAT IS ARTIFICIAL INTELLIGENCE? 4
    DEFINING AI 4
    FROM ANCIENT HISTORY TO THE PRESENT DAY 6
    THE 1950S 7
    THE 1960S 8
    THE 1970S 12
    THE 1980S 13
    THE 1990S 14
    THE 2000S 15
    THE 2010S 16
    THE 2020S 19

CHAPTER 3 22

HOW AI WORKS: THE BUILDING BLOCKS OF INTELLIGENCE 22
    DATA: FOOD FOR THE AI BRAIN 23
    PROGRAMS AND ALGORITHMS 26

CHAPTER 4 32

MACHINE LEARNING AND DEEP LEARNING 32
    MACHINE LEARNING EXPLAINED 32
    MACHINE LEARNING METHODS 33
    APPLYING ML 34
    DEEP LEARNING 35

CHAPTER 5 38

FROM THE MOUTHS OF EXPERTS 38
    SAM ALTMAN, OPENAI'S CEO 38
    ELON MUSK, FOUNDER OF TESLA 38
    YOSHUA BENGIO, DEEP LEARNING PIONEER 39
    "THE GODFATHER OF DEEP LEARNING" GEOFFREY HINTON 40
    FEI-FEI LI, CO-DIRECTOR OF STANFORD'S AI LAB 40
    ANDREW NG, GOOGLE BRAIN CO-FOUNDER 41
    DEMIS HASSABIS, DEEPMIND'S CEO 41

- Cynthia Breazeal, Creator of Jibo 42
- Eliezer Yudkowsky, Machine Intelligence Research Institute 42
- Ilya Sutskever, Co-Founder of OpenAI 43
- Satya Nadella, CEO of Microsoft 43
- Yann LeCun, Facebook AI Research 43
- Mo Gawdat, Former Chief Business Officer, Google X 44

CHAPTER 6 45

APPLICATIONS OF AI 45

- AI at Home 45
- AI in Healthcare 47
- Environmental Protection and Sustainability 49

CHAPTER 7 52

ETHICAL CONSIDERATIONS IN AI 52

- AI Bias 52
- Transparency 53
- Job Loss 53
- AI Safety 54

CHAPTER 8 55

THE FUTURE OF AI 55

- Towards AGI and Superintelligence 58

CHAPTER 9 61

RESOURCES FOR YOUR AI JOURNEY 61

- Online Courses and Tutorials 61
- YouTube Channels and Podcasts 63
- Websites and Blogs 64
- Software and Tools 64
- Competitions and Hackathons 65
- Community and Networking 66
- A Final Word 70

Chapter 1

Introduction

Welcome to the World of AI

Welcome to "AI for Smart Pre-Teens and Teens Ages 10-19". Are you ready to embark on an exciting voyage through the fascinating realm of AI? We will be unraveling its secrets, possibilities, and impact on our lives and learning more about its inner workings. This book is designed to interest and excite readers who are in their pre-teen and teenage years. Whether you're a tech fanatic, a curious mind, or simply want to comprehend the technologies impacting our future, you will find this book to be an ideal companion. If you have read my previous book, "AI for Smart Kids Ages 6-9", you are already well prepared. There are some differences you will notice in this book. Firstly, the writing style is at the appropriate level for more advanced readers. Many of the core ideas in AI will be explained with more detail and precision. We will also touch upon more advanced concepts in AI, and go into those in more technical detail as well. There will also be some detailed examples, and plenty of resources you can dive into in order to expand your horizons further. These are meant to sharpen your critical thinking skills and explore new directions and opportunities in the field of artificial intelligence. If you find that the content in this book is too complex, here is what I suggest. Read the book "AI for Smart Kids Ages 6-9" first, and a couple of months later, come back to this book to see the difference. If you are a teacher using this book in the classroom, you can read through both books to see which one is more suitable for the kids in your class. Now that we are done with the preamble, let's get on to the main content of this book! And yes, this book is also suitable for adult readers who would like to learn about AI.

The term "artificial intelligence," or AI for short, has quickly become embedded in today's contemporary discourse. AI is present in many aspects of our daily lives, including voice assistants such as Siri and Alexa, self-driving cars, and personalized suggestions on streaming platforms. But what precisely does "AI" stand for? How does it work? And what are its capabilities? These are the questions that will guide our discussion moving forward. We will also discover the potentially life-changing abilities that AI can confer on humans, as well as the dangers that AI poses to us if it is not used correctly.

AI, which stands for "artificial intelligence," is no longer just a term used in science fiction or for describing advanced robots. It is seamlessly integrated into our lives, and affects how we work, play, and learn. But why does it matter that you know about AI? The answer is simple: AI is becoming a bigger part of our lives, so learning about it can help you in your work, hobbies, and future career. Knowing about AI can help you figure out why certain things on your devices and online happen the way they do. For example, have you ever thought about how your social media feeds seem to know exactly what you like? Or how can your digital assistant understand what you say and do what you ask? That's AI in action. It is the technology behind recommendation algorithms, voice recognition, and a lot of other things. By learning about AI, you can get a better handle on the digital world around you. This will make you a knowledgeable and savvy tech user.

More importantly, AI is going to be a big part of many jobs and industries when you get older. AI is changing the way we do everything, from medicine and farming to entertainment and education. It makes routine tasks easier by automating them, helps us analyze large amounts of data, and even lets us solve hard problems. If you learn about AI now, you will be ahead of the game in the future. You will be better prepared for the jobs of the future, and you might even find or create new career paths you (or anyone else for that matter) had never thought of before.

You should also know that AI isn't just for computer scientists and engineers. AI is helping artists make beautiful works of art. AI is helping writers come up with new ideas and stories. AI is helping doctors diagnose diseases and come up with new ways to treat them. Even farmers are using AI to keep an eye on their crops and get the most out of them. So, no matter what you want to be when you grow up, AI will probably be a part of it. Just think of how we use computers connected to the Internet today. It is not just computer scientists and engineers who use them; literally every member of society and every type of organization and business would find themselves lost without the ability to go online. The same is the case with AI - it is going to permeate our lives in ways we haven't thought of before. By knowing how to harness the powers of AI, you can be more creative, get more done, and have a bigger impact in your field.

However, there is more to artificial intelligence than just its scientific and practical applications. It also raises profound questions about the nature of what we do and what potential harm can come from the use of such a technology. We will therefore also investigate the moral questions and ethical conundrums that come up as a result of developing and utilizing AI, as well as debate the obligations that come along with it.

Towards the end of this book, I will provide activities, hands-on experiences, and links to websites and resources that will inspire you to explore the field of artificial intelligence on your own. We will go through the fundamentals of programming and algorithms and the role they have played in the evolution of AI. We will also discuss techniques like machine learning, deep learning, and neural nets, all of which will equip you with the skills necessary to develop your own artificial intelligence projects. In addition, we will discuss the numerous employment opportunities available in AI as well as ways that you might launch your own adventure in the field of AI.

So, tell me, are you up for an exciting new experience? Join me on an exciting journey into the world of artificial intelligence (AI), where we'll solve the riddles of this ground-breaking technology and uncover the ways in which it has the potential to alter our future.

Chapter 2

What Is Artificial Intelligence?

Defining AI

Let us start by defining our topic of interest. Artificial Intelligence, more commonly abbreviated to AI, is a subfield of computer science that focuses on the development of intelligent machines that are able to carry out activities that would normally require the intelligence of a human being. The idea of having some sort of "artificial intelligence", i.e., a non-human entity displaying intelligence, has captivated our collective imagination for centuries, but its journey from the realm of fiction to a reality we interact with daily is a remarkable one. In this chapter, we will explore the types of AI, the fascinating history of AI, and trace its origins and major milestones that have shaped the field into what it is today.

Firstly, you should know that not all types of AI are the same. We recognize a few different types of AI. Let us consider each of the major types of AI and see how they differ.

Narrow AI

Narrow AI, commonly referred to as weak AI, excels at a single, specifically targeted task. It can be compared to a computer program that lacks broad intelligence and is optimized for mastery of a single skill, like playing chess. Similar to a chess engine that has thoroughly analyzed previous games and developed strategic heuristics, narrow AI is excellent within its designated competency but is limited outside of it.

For instance, using training data, an image recognition algorithm designed to recognize cats in photos may quickly determine whether or not a particular image contains a cat. However, it is limited to cat recognition and cannot ascertain the presence of additional things in an image or carry out any related analytical activities.

General AI

General AI, commonly referred to as strong AI, strives for human-level comprehension and adaptability across fields. It aims to mimic a variety of cognitive functions possessed by humans, including language processing, learning, and reasoning. It has a holistic aptitude for gaining large domains of knowledge and using them flexibly, as opposed to concentrating on specific tasks.

For instance, a general AI trained on the chess rules can quickly understand and master the games of checkers, go, and other similar rule-based domains without the need for explicit training in them by applying its knowledge of strategy, opponent modeling, and probabilistic thinking. It may combine and expand on knowledge already known, displaying generalist intelligence. Its capacity to comprehend contextual knowledge, adhere to logical reasoning, and continuously learn from experience sets it apart from narrow AI.

Superintelligence

Last but not least, superintelligence is the term used to describe hypothetical AI systems that, across a wide variety of cognitive tasks, greatly outperform all human capabilities. Superintelligence intends to be able to tackle complex problems that are currently insurmountable for humans, such as climate change, sickness, and poverty, by recursively self-improving and utilizing the wealth of data and processing capacity.

Superintelligence creation, however, continues to be a difficult technical task due to worries about ethical and existential risk. At the current stage of AI development, ongoing research by academia and the private sector aims to create safe and helpful superintelligence, although this remains theoretical.

From Ancient History to the Present Day

The concept of intelligent machines can be traced back to ancient times, when myths and stories depicted artificial beings with human-like abilities. One such example is the ancient Greek myth of Hephaestus, the god of craftsmen, who created mechanical servants to assist him. One could think of them as an early form of robot! In another example, again from Greek mythology, the immensely talented artisan Daedalus built the Labyrinth to enclose the Minotaur, a strange beast with a human body and a bull's head. No one was able to effectively escape the Labyrinth because of its intricate layout and difficulty. These stories demonstrate the idea of making complex constructions or puzzles with a certain level of intelligence, which is similar to the difficulties encountered when designing AI systems. Though these stories are not connected to the power of computers per se, these early tales reflected humanity's fascination with the idea of creating intelligent beings and systems.

A number of smart inventors began to consider how such machines might in fact make it to reality, and as more progress was made, several new ideas came to the surface. Charles Babbage created the Difference Engine in 1833. This was a primitive mechanical calculator, but one of the first attempts to create a machine that would "compute". He then worked on the Analytical Engine, a more sophisticated mechanical computer that could perform a variety of tasks. Another brilliant mind, Ada Lovelace, published her notes on the Analytical Engine in 1843, and these included the first algorithm that a machine could process. She is frequently regarded as the first computer programmer because of this. We will talk later about the importance of algorithms in computer science in general and AI in particular.

However, it wasn't until the 20th century that AI began to take shape as a scientific discipline. This is when AI as an area of research and application really took off, and many important advances were made. Let us look at the key epochs in AI history where major contributions were made to the field:

The 1950s

The study of artificial intelligence, or AI, was in its infancy in the 1950s. British physicist Alan Turing initially conceived of the concept of artificial intelligence in 1936, when he talked about the notion of computability. In the 1940s, he went on to crack the famous Enigma code during World War II, leading to the development of early computing machines. He had famous contemporaries like John Von Neumann and Claude Shannon, who also made major advances in the fields of computer hardware, information theory, and computer architecture.

Turing's early ideas became so important that he is credited as being the father of AI. He created the now-famous Turing Test to determine whether a machine could act so intelligently as to be indistinguishable from a person. Consider the following scenario: You are interacting with two players in different rooms, one of whom is a machine and the other is a person. The Turing Test is passed if the machine can persuade you that it is a human. Because it switched the emphasis from building machines that could think to building machines that could behave like humans, this idea was groundbreaking.

Fig. Alan Turing, hard at work (Source: The Harvard Gazette)

John McCarthy, a mathematics professor, officially created the phrase "Artificial Intelligence" in 1956 during a conference held at Dartmouth College. The birth of artificial intelligence as a formal field of research is often credited to this conference. The symposium's goal was to look into the idea that every aspect of learning or intelligence may be so precisely defined that a machine could replicate it.

Marvin Minsky, Allen Newell, and Herbert Simon were three computer scientists who eventually rose to prominence in the field of artificial intelligence. And they were among the attendees at the seminal Dartmouth Conference. Marvin Minsky, for instance, later co-founded the renowned MIT Media Lab and authored several important publications on artificial intelligence.

The initial artificial intelligence software was also created at this time. Even though they were rather primitive by today's standards, they were capable of breakthrough activities like playing checkers, solving problems, and proving mathematical theorems.

The 1950s were a significant decade for AI because they heralded several new ideas and launched the careers of several brilliant visionaries who would go on to have a deep impact on the field. These developments laid the groundwork for today's rapid advancements in AI.

The 1960s

The rapid development of new ideas in computing led to greater involvement by the US government, as these had major implications for economic and military superiority. Financial support from the US Department of Defense helped the field of AI grow quickly in the 1960s. Due to this funding, LISP and IPL, the first AI programming languages, were developed. John McCarthy at MIT created LISP, which stands for "LISt Processing," and it was developed exclusively for AI study. McCarthy intended LISP to be a tool for exploring and experimenting with new ideas in artificial intelligence. The "Information Processing Language," or IPL, was a different early programming language that had an impact on the creation of AI. These languages represented a significant advancement in AI research since they allowed for the creation of more sophisticated AI programs.

During this period, symbolic techniques and problem-solving were the main topics of AI study. In symbolic approaches, symbols serve as representations of problems and then serve as tools for developing solutions.

Take the following word puzzle as an example: "Sally has twice as many apples as Tom. How many apples does Sally have if Tom has 'x'? You already know how to solve this simple problem if you know how to use your intuition. But how do we teach a computer to solve such problems without any assistance? Well, we just try to teach the computer to think in terms of symbols. You already know how to use these techniques under another name: algebra.

An algebraic symbol, such as "x," can stand in for the unknown quantity (in this case, the number of apples Tom has). Then, using this symbol, we can create an equation to describe the issue: "Sally has 2 times "x" apples." You can write this equation as "S = 2x," where S stands for how many apples Sally owns. We can now manipulate this equation to obtain the solution using algebraic principles. In this instance, we're looking for the value of 'x', which stands for Tom's apple count. "S/2 = x" allows for the division of both sides by 2. solutions, We can deduce from this calculation that Tom has half as many apples as Sally does. We need more data or numbers to determine the precise number of apples. Assume we are aware that Sally has 10 apples. When we enter this number into the equation, we receive the result "10/2 = x," which is then reduced to "5 = x." Tom now has five apples.

This example shows how equations can be changed to discover solutions, and symbols (like "x") are used to represent unknown quantities. It is comparable to how you are taught algebra in school, where variables are represented by letters, and students learn how to solve equations to determine the values of those variables. Algebra and symbolic methods both use symbols to express issues and as instruments for creating solutions. Of course, with computers, we can rapidly expand the number of variables and solve all kinds of tricky equations. While humans may stumble once the number of variables and variations increases, computers don't get tired and have vast amounts of processing power. This method was used to develop AI programs that could play games like checkers, solve mathematical puzzles, and even imitate how humans solve problems.

The first AI laboratories were also established in the 1960s at MIT and Stanford. These labs served as computer scientists' playgrounds, allowing them to test out novel concepts and create the first applications of artificial intelligence. The General Problem Solver (GPS), created at this time by Allen Newell and Herbert Simon, is one of the most renowned programs. GPS was created to resemble how people solve problems. It would divide an issue into smaller components, address each component, and then bring the many answers together to address the entire problem. This was significant because it was one of the first systems to be able to approach complex issues in a manner that was comparable to that of people.

Joseph Weizenbaum at MIT created the computer program ELIZA, which was another significant innovation. One of the earliest algorithms capable of understanding natural language, ELIZA could comprehend user input and respond to it in a manner resembling human conversation. The "DOCTOR" script in ELIZA is most notable for simulating a psychotherapist and giving some users the impression that they are speaking to a real person.

Here is a brief example of a dialogue generated by the 1960s-era natural language processing tool ELIZA:

> User: Good day, ELIZA. How are you doing today?
>
> ELIZA: Hello. I automatically respond to commands. How do you feel right now?
>
> User: I've been experiencing some stress lately.
>
> ELIZA: Why do you believe you're under stress?
>
> User: My workload at work is excessive because I have so many deadlines.
>
> ELIZA: Please elaborate on these deadlines. How do you feel about them?
>
> User: I feel like I'm constantly under pressure and can't keep up.
>
> ELIZA: You seem to be under a great deal of pressure. How do you usually handle such circumstances?

User: I attempt to prioritize chores and divide them into more manageable chunks whenever possible.

ELIZA: It can be beneficial to divide jobs into smaller steps. Are there any other things that make you stressed out?

User: Sometimes, I worry about making mistakes and feel inadequate.

ELIZA: It's normal to worry about making mistakes and to have self-doubt. Everybody makes errors, so take advantage of the chance to improve. Do you have any further information to share?

User: I appreciate your patience, ELIZA. To talk about it feels fantastic.

ELIZA: Thank you very much. I'm here to talk and assist you. Keep in mind that discussing your emotions might be helpful. Are you thinking of anything else right now?

What do you think of this conversation? It looks convincing, doesn't it? You will be surprised to know that rather than truly understanding the dialogue, ELIZA's responses were determined by simplistic pattern matching criteria. By mirroring the user's words and urging more emotional investigation, it attempted to mimic a psychotherapist. Despite its simple interface and abilities, ELIZA amazed a lot of people. It seemed like it was making science fiction a reality!

Thus, the 1960s were a decade of rapid research and development in AI. The foundation for the future of AI was being built through the creation of AI programming languages, the construction of AI labs, and the development of applications like GPS and ELIZA. These developments helped us get a step closer to realizing our vision of building machines that think and communicate like people.

The 1970s

The first "AI winter," was a time when funding and interest in AI research declined, and occurred in the 1970s. This occurred as a result of the 1960s' lofty expectations for AI's potential and the slow pace of technological advancement. Large AI programs couldn't be run on computers because they were still highly expensive and lacked the necessary processing power. Additionally, many of the issues that scientists were attempting to tackle turned out to be more complicated than they previously believed.

However, despite these difficulties, AI development continued. In reality, it changed course and began to move in the direction of knowledge-based systems. These systems were created to use a massive quantity of information on a particular subject to solve challenging problems. They analyzed the data and developed answers using logic and rules.

MYCIN and DENDRAL were two of the best-known knowledge-based systems created at this time. MYCIN was created at Stanford University with the goal of identifying bacterial illnesses and advising on the best course of action. It was one of the earliest programs to use rule-based systems, a type of artificial intelligence where a set of rules is provided for the program to follow while making decisions.

On the other hand, DENDRAL was a system created to examine the chemical makeup of molecules. DENDRAL, which was created at Stanford University as well, employed a set of principles to forecast potential organic molecule structures using mass spectrometry data. This was an important advancement in AI since it demonstrated how AI technologies could be applied to actual scientific challenges.

The 1970s were a difficult yet crucial decade for AI. Despite the initial AI winter, researchers kept challenging the limits of what AI was capable of. The creation of knowledge-based systems like MYCIN and DENDRAL demonstrated how AI might be used to address challenging issues in fields like chemistry and medicine.

The 1980s

The 1980s saw a resurgence of interest in artificial intelligence. This was partially a result of increased research funding and the emergence of machine learning as a new AI strategy. Machine learning systems are intended to learn from data and enhance their performance over time, in contrast to the rule-based systems of the 1970s. The fact that AI systems could adapt and gain knowledge from their experiences, much like people do, was a game-changer.

The backpropagation algorithm was one of the major advancements that made this possible. Neural networks, which are computer systems based on the human brain, are trained using the backpropagation technique. In order to change the weights of the connections between the neurons in the network, the algorithm first measures the error in the output of the network. The network improves at delivering the required output with each iteration of this procedure, which is repeated numerous times. The development of backpropagation made it possible to train increasingly complex, multi-layer neural networks, which in turn made deep learning possible.

Deep learning is a subset of machine learning that makes use of multilayered neural networks. Compared to prior AI systems, these "deep" networks are able to solve more difficult issues and can learn from vast volumes of data. Many of the AI systems that are currently in use, like voice recognition and image identification, use deep learning.

Expert systems, which are AI systems created to mimic human experts' decision-making abilities, were also developed in the 1980s. XCON (short for eXpert CONfigurer) was one of the most well-known expert systems created at this time. The Digital Equipment Corporation created XCON to aid in configuring computer systems. By making decisions utilizing rules and understanding of computer systems, it was able to take the position of human specialists.

In conclusion, the 1980s saw a number of important developments in AI. AI research underwent a change with the emergence of machine learning, the growth of backpropagation, and the development of expert systems. These innovations paved the way for the tremendous advancements in AI we observe today and brought us one step closer to our goal of developing AI systems that can learn and make judgments similarly to humans.

The 1990s

With the birth of intelligent agents and multi-agent systems, the 1990s saw a fast rise and progress in AI. A system that can understand its surroundings and take actions to accomplish its objectives is an intelligent agent. Multiple intelligent agents work together in multi-agent systems to complete tasks. Problems that are challenging or impossible for a single agent or monolithic system to solve can be solved with these systems. These systems' creation signaled a significant milestone in AI by enabling more sophisticated and adaptable AI applications.

During this time, the internet began to take off, which significantly affected AI. Web-based AI applications have been created as a result of the abundance of data available on the internet that might be utilized to train AI systems. These programs could exploit data from the internet to offer services like search engines and recommendation systems, among others.

When IBM's Deep Blue, a chess-playing computer, defeated Garry Kasparov in 1997, it was one of the most significant events of the 1990s. Deep Blue was a supercomputer that played chess using both strategy and brute force. A team of chess grandmasters created a very sophisticated evaluation function for it, and it was capable of evaluating 200 million positions per second. An important turning point in the development of AI was the triumph of Deep Blue versus Kasparov, which demonstrated that an AI system could surpass a human in a challenging endeavor.

In conclusion, the 1990s saw a number of important developments in AI. A change in AI capabilities was brought about by the creation of intelligent agents, multi-agent systems, and web-based AI applications, as well as by Deep Blue's win. AI developed from the idea of artificial intelligence (AI) in the 1950s to the reality of intelligent systems that can learn and make decisions in the 1990s. Despite times of declining funding and attention, ongoing advances in AI created the foundation for the AI technology we use today.

The 2000s

The AI field underwent major transformation in the 2000s, with an emphasis placed on developing useful applications that could be applied in daily life. Machine learning methods, such as deep learning and reinforcement learning, also advanced quickly during this time.

A sort of machine learning called reinforcement learning teaches an agent to decide by acting in the environment to accomplish a goal. The agent receives rewards or consequences for its actions, and over time, it develops the ability to make wiser judgments. From video games to robots, this kind of learning is applied in a variety of contexts.

On the other hand, deep learning is a branch of machine learning that is based on multiple-layer artificial neural networks. These deep neural networks can learn from a massive quantity of data and are built to mimic how the human brain functions. Due to its capacity to generate extremely accurate results, particularly when working with huge and complicated datasets, deep learning gained popularity in the 2000s.

When Stanford's autonomous vehicle, Stanley, won the DARPA Grand Challenge in 2005, it marked a significant turning point in the development of artificial intelligence. Without the aid of anyone, Stanley was able to go 131 miles across the desert. This was a noteworthy accomplishment since it demonstrated that AI systems were capable of navigating challenging real-world conditions. In order to understand its surroundings and make judgments, Stanley made use of a variety of AI techniques, including computer vision and machine learning.

Geoffrey Hinton, referred to as the "godfather of deep learning," and his students first used the phrase "deep learning" in the machine learning field in 2006. Hinton's work on deep learning algorithms, particularly the backpropagation technique for training multi-layer neural networks, had a significant influence on deep learning. Due to their capacity for processing massive quantities of data and generating incredibly precise results—outperforming other machine learning models in tasks like speech and picture recognition—deep learning models have begun to gain popularity.

In conclusion, the 2000s saw tremendous advancement and real-world use of AI. The development of cutting-edge machine learning techniques and the completion of significant milestones like the DARPA Grand Challenge serve as proof that AI has the ability to solve challenging, real-world problems.

The 2010s

The 2010s were a decade in which AI technology began to permeate our daily lives. One of the most significant occasions was when IBM's Watson triumphed on the renowned game show Jeopardy! in 2011. Watson is a question-response computer system that employs machine learning and natural language processing to comprehend and respond to queries. Being successful on Jeopardy! was an important accomplishment because it proved that artificial intelligence (AI) systems could comprehend and analyze natural language at a level comparable to humans.

By utilizing a deep learning model, the Alex Krizhevsky and Geoffrey Hinton-led team won the ImageNet competition in 2012. The challenge involved picture recognition. They employed a deep convolutional neural network model called AlexNet. Deep learning models called convolutional neural networks (CNNs) are very effective at processing images. Because it demonstrated that deep learning models might perform better than conventional machine learning models in challenging tasks like image identification, winning the ImageNet competition was a watershed moment for AI.

Over the course of the decade, AI began to appear in a variety of applications. Voice assistants like Siri and Alexa use AI to recognize and carry out speech commands. Netflix and Amazon use AI in their recommendation systems to look at your viewing and purchasing history and make suggestions for products or movies you might like.

During the 2010s, self-driving automobile development made major strides as well. On public highways, businesses like Tesla and Waymo began testing driverless vehicles. To navigate the roadways and make driving judgments, these vehicles use a variety of AI technologies, including computer vision, sensor data processing, and machine learning.

The pace of advancement didn't stop there. One of the best Go players in the world, Lee Sedol, competed against AlphaGo, a Google subsidiary's computer program, in March 2016, and the AI won! This event has been compared by many to the 'Sputnik moment' or the 'Apollo moment', both of which signified tremendous change and technological investment by the superpowers in the decades ahead.

You might be asking, What is so amazing about a computer program winning a game? Haven't we been there before with chess? However, the board game of Go is much more tricky to play than chess. Its total possible moves exceed the number of atoms in the cosmos! Go calls for intuition, inventiveness, and strategic thinking, in contrast to chess or checkers, where computers may beat humans with calculating power alone. Because of Go's extreme intricacy, humans were long believed to be invincible. AlphaGo, however, changed all that. It employed a ground-breaking technique called deep learning, which allowed it to learn and advance by competing against itself in many games.

A Completed Go Game

Let us look at Go a little closer. Go, a well-known board game for two players that has its roots in ancient China, is played by millions of players worldwide, and is very popular in Asia. Territorial control, strategy, and tactics are the key components of the game. Here is a brief explanation:

- Go is played on a square board with a grid of lines that is typically 19x19, though novices may also use boards that are 9x9 or 13x13 in size.
- The pieces, known as stones, are placed on the intersections of the lines by each player in turn.

- By the end of the game, you want to have more control over the board than your opponent has.
- By carefully encircling their opponent's stones with their own stones, players can surround and seize their opponent's stones. Stones that are captured are taken from the board.
- The game is over when both players decide there are no more viable movements or when both players pass their turns in a row. At that point, the players count the area they have successfully controlled.
- The person with the most territory wins the game!

Despite having straightforward rules which you can understand almost instantly, the game of go has intricate strategic elements that make it exciting and difficult for players of various ability levels to master.

The world was shocked when AlphaGo defeated Lee Sedol in a matchup by winning four out of five games. For several reasons, this triumph was a significant turning point for AI. Firstly, it showed off the amazing capabilities of machine learning algorithms. Instead of relying on pre-programmed plans, AlphaGo learned and developed on its own, coming up with novel strategies and unexpected plays that even the top human players hadn't considered. Rather than studying past games, AlphaGo played millions of games against itself and began to formulate its own 'understanding' of Go.

Second, it demonstrated AI's potential to solve complex issues in the real world that were previously thought to be the domain of human intelligence alone. Go has practical uses in areas like medicine, economics, and military strategy in addition to being just a game. AlphaGo demonstrated that AI may help with these problems by being exceptionally good at the game of Go.

Third, the triumph of AlphaGo spurred a global resurgence in interest in AI research and development. It inspired researchers and engineers to push the limits of what AI is capable of. It also encouraged young brains, like yours, to research AI and think about the potential it offers for influencing the future.

AlphaGo's triumph against a human opponent represented a significant advancement in AI. It showed off the effectiveness of machine learning, highlighted the promise of AI in solving challenging issues, and motivated a new generation of researchers and enthusiasts to investigate the potential of artificial intelligence. We can safely say that the 2010s were a decade in which AI began to permeate our daily lives and establish itself in our collective imagination. AI technologies have proven their ability to handle difficult jobs and simplify our lives by winning game shows and driving cars.

Here is a tip: if you get a chance, watch the documentary AlphaGo with your family (available on YouTube and other streaming services). You will be amazed at the kind of attention and coverage this contest between Lee Sedol and AlphaGo generated.

The 2020s

In the 2020s, AI is beginning to play a significant role in a wide range of industries, with big corporations like Google, Amazon, Microsoft, IBM, and Facebook driving AI research and development.

AI is being applied to healthcare to anticipate illness outbreaks, aid in diagnosis, and tailor treatment regimens. With initiatives like forecasting patient deterioration and protein folding, businesses like Google's DeepMind are making progress in the application of AI to healthcare.

AI algorithms are used in finance to automate trading, control risk, and forecast market movements. Businesses like IBM and their Watson platform are leading the introduction of AI to the financial sector. AI is being utilized in education to personalize instruction, automate grading, and offer tutoring. Businesses like Carnegie Learning are using AI to offer individualized educational opportunities.

Google's conversational AI technology, Bard, was launched in 2022. LaMDA (Language Model for Dialogue Applications), a sizable language model developed by Google, serves as the foundation for Bard. Bard reflects Google's significant effort in creating conversational AI that can understand context and deliver helpful information, despite being initially error-prone.

In 2022, Microsoft also unveiled Sydney, an AI chatbot that was based on Prometheus, a sizable language model. Sydney strives to have casual interactions and to be a good, honest person.

Anthropic also debuted Claude, an AI assistant, around the same time. Claude is helpful, risk-free, and trustworthy thanks to a cutting-edge AI safety technique called Constitutional AI. Claude is more limited and constrained for safety compared to the LLMs of other firms, which may occasionally respond in damaging or counterproductive ways.

While major tech companies like Google, Microsoft, Meta, and Baidu compete to create the largest, most powerful LLMs, startups like Character.ai and Anthropic are pushing AI conversational interfaces in new and beneficial ways. Future interactions with technology and information appear to increasingly revolve around natural language AI.

However, what really changed the landscape of AI for most people was the introduction and launch of ChatGPT. The creation of GPT-3 by OpenAI, a company Elon Musk initially co-founded, can be considered one of the most important developments in AI. Generative Pretrained Transformer 3 (GPT-3) is a language prediction model that employs machine learning to create text that resembles that of a human. It can perform things like translate, respond to inquiries, and even compose poetry. OpenAI introduced ChatGPT in November 2022. The goal of ChatGPT is to conduct casual discussions and respond in a way that is honest, helpful, and safe. Over 1 million users had tested ChatGPT within a few days after its launch, as excitement surged. In fact, ChatGPT became one of the fastest-growing apps in history after accumulating over 100 million users in just two months. People used it for anything from answering inquiries to creating essays and articles because of its human-like conversational ability and broad knowledge on a wide range of topics. ChatGPT thus marked a significant turning point in the public's ability to access and utilize conversational AI.

Today, AI is increasingly being used for data analysis and decision-making. Large datasets are now analyzed, patterns are found, and predictions are made using AI algorithms. This is especially helpful in industries like meteorology, where artificial intelligence is used to forecast weather patterns, and business, where artificial intelligence is used to study consumer behavior and industry trends. There is also a renewed interest in developing humanoid robots that will interact with people, not just industrial robots that will largely remain unseen beyond the public's eyes. Consider this example from August 2023. The Chinese company Unitree Robotics recently announced the development of a humanoid robot, H1. Equipped with 3D lidar and a depth camera for autonomous navigation, H1 stands at 71 inches tall, weighs 100 lbs, and moves at a speed of 3.4mph. Unitree is developing robotic hands for it, aiming for commercialization in the next three to 10 years. The company's quadruped robot 'dog', Go2, is equipped with 4D lidar for versatile navigation and is already available for sale.

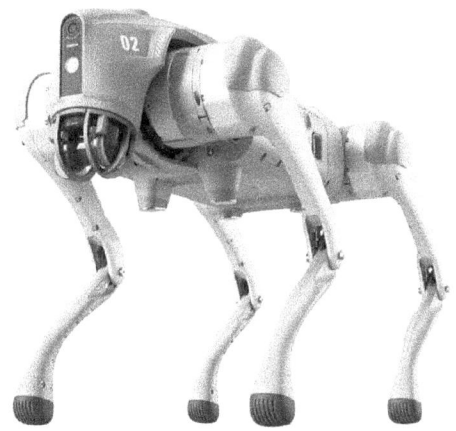

Unitree's Go2 Robot Dog

Despite the breathtaking achievements of AI so far, the extremely rapid development of AI has also brought up significant cultural and ethical challenges. Given that AI systems frequently require enormous volumes of data to operate efficiently, data privacy is a big challenge. Concerns have also been raised regarding how AI may affect employment as it develops the capacity to carry out tasks currently completed by humans. The speed of its adoption has also brought up problems, including the distribution of false information, worries about plagiarism, and the future of work itself.

In conclusion, the decade of the 2020s will see substantial developments in AI. Major corporations are setting the bar for AI research and development, and AI is quickly integrating itself into our culture. Despite these difficulties, AI has the power to fundamentally alter the way we live and work. It's critical to think about the ethical and societal ramifications as we create and improve AI technology and work toward using AI in a way that is beneficial to all.

Chapter 3

How AI Works: The Building Blocks of Intelligence

Now that we have a grasp of what AI is and its potential to revolutionize our lives, let us delve into the inner workings of this fascinating field. In this chapter, we'll explore the building blocks of artificial intelligence and how they come together to create intelligent machines.

We already know that AI is changing everything from self-driving cars to TikTok recommendations. But how does it actually work? As we saw earlier, AI is all about giving machines the ability to learn, kind of like humans do. By looking at large amounts of data, AI can identify patterns and make predictions. Thus, first and foremost, AI needs data to work its magic. And it is not just data, but useful, clean, and structured data that it can work on without confusion. Quality datasets are therefore essential—garbage in, garbage out, as they say. With good data, programmers can give the AI instructions using computer languages like Python. These instructions are called algorithms—think step-by-step recipes for the AI to follow. Different tasks need different algorithms. Then we get to the fun part—machine learning. This lets AI improve on its own without needing new programming. It is as if AI is teaching itself, and it can happen with some human assistance or in a completely independent fashion. When AI is trained on labeled data by humans (say, photos of cats labeled by humans as "cat"), it learns by comparing the labels to its predictions. We call this supervised learning. We can also have a situation where we simply let the AI find patterns in unlabeled data without any guidance. This is 'unsupervised learning', and with today's computational capabilities, we find that this can work very well, much to our surprise.

Other key AI skills include computer vision (recognizing images and videos), natural language processing (understanding language), and deep learning (advanced techniques to handle unstructured data like images and text). With all these powers combined, AI can do some amazing things: drive cars, detect cancer, translate languages, recommend videos, and so much more. The future will have AI built into nearly everything! Let us look at the building blocks of AI, starting with the food that powers it, i.e., data!

Data: Food for the AI Brain

AI algorithms rely extensively on vast datasets in order to learn, improve performance, minimize bias, and operate effectively in the real world. AI models rely on data to learn, inform themselves, and make themselves useful to humans.

During the training phase, AI models require enormous training datasets in order to learn patterns and relationships and make predictions. For instance, ImageNet is the common benchmark dataset for image recognition. By learning from such a broad set of examples, algorithms can build robust models for identifying and classifying objects in images. Speech recognition systems such as Alexa are trained on tens of thousands of hours of labeled audio data to understand natural language. I will provide you with more examples of these datasets below.

Beyond training, maintaining a constant flow of relevant real-world data is critical for AI systems to continuously enhance their capabilities over time through feedback loops. As search engines like Google interact with billions of users worldwide, they accumulate troves of behavioral data on queries, clicks, dwell times, and other signals. This data is used to repeatedly update and refine their ranking algorithms to improve search relevance. Recommendation systems on Netflix, Amazon, and YouTube also ingest endless streams of user data, including views, ratings, and purchases, to keep adapting their models and serving personalized content.

Additionally, it is crucial to use unbiased and representative training data to prevent problems like demographic inequalities and exclusions that AI might unintentionally perpetuate. Facial recognition algorithms have exhibited racial and gender bias, partly due to the overrepresentation of lighter skin tones in training datasets. Diversifying data sources and distributions is thus vital.

Overall, constructing reliable ground truths through extensive, high-quality datasets is integral to training, evaluating, and deploying robust, unbiased AI systems. As computing capabilities expand exponentially, access to abundant data is becoming one of the most significant constraints and competitive differentiators for the advancement of AI. The organizations and nations leading in AI today are those with the resources to capture, curate, and capitalize on data throughout the AI pipeline.

Data is like the food that fuels AI. The more quality data it gets, the smarter it becomes. As I already mentioned, AI uses massive datasets, sometimes with millions of images, texts, or other pieces of information, to find patterns and make predictions. It's like if you studied thousands of flashcards intensely, you'd soon start to recognize them and come up with the correct answers.

Here are some examples of big datasets that are often used to train AI systems and how they can be prepared:

Datasets of Images

ImageNet, which I referred to earlier, has more than 14 million images that have been labeled and put into thousands of groups, such as cars, animals, etc. The images are cleaned by getting rid of corrupt files, made the same size, and organized with annotation files that list the titles for each class.

Datasets of text

Wikipedia is a great example of a large, public dataset containing huge amounts of text. Obviously, the entirety of Wikipedia has a lot of words that need to be cleaned up by getting rid of formatting, correcting spelling mistakes, and making grammar more consistent. The writing can then be broken up into documents, paragraphs, sentences, and words that can be analyzed.

Datasets of Speech

LibriSpeech is an example of an audio database that has thousands of hours of English voice samples that have been labeled. Background noise is taken out of the raw audio, and the speech is turned into writing to make it more organized.

Data from sensors

Sensor data is becoming increasingly important for training AI models. One major source of sensor data is the Internet of Things (IoT). Connected devices with sensors like smartphones, home appliances, vehicles, and industrial equipment generate massive amounts of data. This IoT sensor data can be collected and used to train models in areas like predictive maintenance, autonomous vehicles, smart homes, and more. Another key source is specialized sensor hardware. Companies are producing sensors for capturing audio, video, temperature, motion, pressure, and more. Deploying a network of custom sensors provides reliable data for environments like factories, farms, and cities. The scale of the data generated makes it suitable to train robust deep learning models. However, the hardware cost can be a barrier.

Public data sets with sensor feeds are freely available for some domains. In autonomous driving, there are lidar and camera data sets for urban driving. Lidar sensors are an invaluable source of data for training robust AI models. Lidar uses pulsed lasers to precisely map physical environments in 3D. Self-driving companies heavily rely on lidar arrays mounted on vehicles to capture point cloud data of their surroundings. For autonomous navigation capabilities, lidar's high-resolution spatial and depth perception is essential. Public driving datasets with lidar feeds provide extensive labeled examples of real-world road conditions to train perception models. While costly, lidar provides indispensable 3D mapping not possible with passive cameras alone. With hardware costs falling and abundant data availability, lidar is becoming more accessible. The rich, detailed scans from lidar remain the gold standard for training AI models for accurate object detection and scene understanding in robotics and autonomous systems.

When creating datasets for AI, we need to ensure that the data itself is usable by the AI. Hence, we need to take steps to:

- Get rid of bad, duplicate, or useless information.
- Organize and label the material so that computers can figure out what it is.
- Put things in a standard format
- Put the data into training, test, and confirmation sets (these are partitions we create, each for a different purpose).

AI models can find useful patterns and make better predictions when they have a lot of clean, structured data to work with. Since the rule of "garbage in, garbage out" always applies, data preparation is a very important step.

Programs and Algorithms

AI uses programs and algorithms to make machines act intelligently. An algorithm is like a recipe that tells a computer exactly what steps to take to solve a problem or complete a task. AI programmers write complicated code containing many algorithms that train computers to do human-like things.

For example, deep learning uses neural networks, which are layers of algorithms that can analyze data to recognize patterns, like identifying a dog in a photo. Programmers build these networks using code in languages like Python and frameworks like TensorFlow. All the math and logic that go into training the AI are implemented through software programs. Another example is natural language processing, which uses algorithms to understand and generate human language.

Programs encode rules about grammar, word meanings, and sentence structure to translate text between languages or interpret commands.

So at their core, AI systems are just code containing algorithms to crunch data, find patterns, make predictions, plan actions, and mimic human intelligence in different ways. Better algorithms lead to smarter AI. As programmers come up with improved techniques for machine learning, reasoning, robotics, and more, AI capabilities grow more advanced.

Major tech companies like Google and Meta have teams of expert programmers developing novel algorithms and modeling them in software to create more capable AI assistants, self-driving cars, recommendation engines, and much more. The algorithms powering AI represent some of the most complex software ever created.

Therefore, despite the fact that AI appears intelligent on the surface, it is really just very complex computer code that programmers have created to mimic human cognition and carry out tasks in an intelligent manner. The skills of the programmers in translating algorithms into code are key to unlocking the potential of artificial intelligence.

How Algorithms Work

The core of computer science and the basis of all digital technology are algorithms. They are a set of guidelines that show a computer how to carry out a task or address a challenge. Then again, why are algorithms so magical?

Consider yourself engaged in a game of chess. You're strategizing, planning your attack and defense, and thinking several moves ahead. The operation of an algorithm is comparable to this. Making calculations follows a set process, whether it's figuring out the fastest way to get where you're going or suggesting a Spotify song you might like.

Design of Algorithms

A series of steps make up the specific structure of an algorithm. Calculations, comparisons, or conditional statements may be used in each step, which is carried out in a specific order. Imagine it as a recipe that instructs the computer how to operate.

For illustration, suppose you have an algorithm to determine the highest number in a list. The format could be as follows:

> 1. Begin with the first number on the list and set it as the highest value to be stored.
>
> 2. Contrast the current figure with the highest.
>
> 3. Update the maximum to the current number if the current number exceeds the maximum.
>
> 4. For each number on the list, repeat steps 2 and 3 once more.
>
> 5. The final value kept in the maximum variable is the maximum number.

As we can see, the algorithm essentially decomposes the problem into parts (sequencing, selection, and iteration) and has feedback mechanisms in place so that it can run through the entire dataset without errors.

Types of Algorithms

Based on their function and behavior, algorithms can be divided into various types. Let's look at some typical types:

> 1. Sorting algorithms, like the one we discussed above, place data in a particular order, such as alphabetical or numerical. Examples include quicksort, bubble sort, and insertion sort.
>
> 2. Searching Algorithms: These algorithms assist us in locating particular data within a sizable dataset. They can be helpful for tasks like looking up a specific item in a list or conducting an internet search. Hash tables, binary search, and linear search are some examples.

3. Pathfinding Algorithms: These algorithms determine the shortest route through a network or graph between two points. They can be used in video games, logistics planning, and navigation systems. Dijkstra's algorithm and A* search are two examples.

4. Machine Learning Algorithms: Without explicit programming, these algorithms allow computers to learn from data and make predictions or decisions. They are essential in fields like recommendation systems, natural language processing, and image recognition. Examples include neural networks, decision trees, and linear regression.

Practical Applications of Algorithms

Algorithms play an important role in our daily lives. Though often invisible to users, algorithms enable many technologies we rely on by crunching data to provide useful output. We can now consider the broad applicability of algorithms through examples in recommendation systems, web search, computer vision, natural language processing, logistics, healthcare, and finance.

Recommendation Systems

From online shopping to social media, recommendation systems utilizing algorithms suggest customized content for each user. Netflix and Amazon analyze our viewing and purchase history to recommend new movies, shows, or products we may enjoy. Facebook prioritizes which posts to display on our feed based on past engagement. Google tailors search results by location, past queries, and sites visited. The sophisticated algorithms powering recommendations deliver more relevant experiences.

Web Search

Google's core search algorithms analyze the billions of web pages to interpret page content, rank authority, and return the most relevant results for search queries in milliseconds. From spell check to autocomplete suggestions, Google's algorithms aim to understand user intent and satisfy their information needs quickly. Search engines have become vital gateways to online information thanks to the algorithms under the hood.

Computer Vision

Algorithms enable machines to interpret and analyze visual data. Face detection algorithms can identify individuals in photos. Object detection helps self-driving cars analyze road conditions. Image classification algorithms categorize photos by their contents. By mimicking human vision, these algorithms are transforming tasks like medical imaging, manufacturing monitoring, and assisting visually impaired users.

Natural Language Processing

Algorithms empower machines to understand, interpret, and generate human language. Voice assistants like Alexa use speech recognition algorithms to convert spoken commands to text. Google Translate applies algorithms to automatically translate between over 100 languages. Sentiment analysis classifies text by emotional tone. From chatbots to predictive text, NLP algorithms enable more natural human-computer interaction.

Logistics

Route optimization algorithms arrange the most efficient routes for delivery trucks to serve multiple addresses. Ride-sharing services like Uber use algorithms to match drivers with riders requesting a pickup. Traffic prediction algorithms used by transportation agencies help drivers avoid congestion. By optimizing logistics, these algorithms provide greener transportation and increase productivity.

Healthcare

Algorithms aid diagnosis by analyzing scans and data for anomalies. Natural language processing interprets clinical notes and medical histories. Algorithms also support personalized medicine by matching treatments to patients. Applied ethically, healthcare algorithms promise earlier disease intervention and improved patient outcomes.

Finance

Some algorithms look through customer info to catch sketchy purchases or transfers that might be fraud. Other algorithms scan the stock market super fast to jump on good trades and make money for traders. There are also algorithms that give you custom tips on how to invest and save money based on your situation. Algorithms thus bring automation and smarts to finance to speed things up and make them more secure.

As we can see from the many examples above, algorithms broadly impact our lives by powering essential technologies and services, from search engines to recommendation systems. As algorithms grow more sophisticated, they will unlock innovations across even more domains. However, the ethical application of algorithms will remain critical. When thoughtfully developed and applied, algorithms have huge potential to improve human society.

Chapter 4

Machine Learning and Deep Learning

In this chapter, we will delve into the basics of Machine Learning, also known as ML, and Deep Learning, which relies on neural networks. Both these ideas are at the core of how artificial intelligence really works in practice.

Machine Learning Explained

The concept of Machine Learning dates back to the 1950s, when pioneers like Arthur Samuel and Alan Turing began exploring the idea of computers learning from data. Since then, Machine Learning has evolved significantly, driven by advancements in computing power, the availability of large datasets, and breakthroughs in algorithms and techniques.

First and foremost, machine learning starts with data. Lots and lots of data! For example, say we want to teach a computer to recognize different types of dogs. We need to feed the computer tons of photos of all kinds of dogs - big dogs, small dogs, dogs of every breed and color. The more data the better! Next, that data gets labeled. Each photo gets tagged as a certain breed of dog so the computer knows "This is a poodle," "This is a bulldog," and so on. This labeled data is called training data because it trains the machine learning model.

Then the exciting part happens - the computer uses this training data to learn on its own! Through complicated math algorithms, it analyzes all the photos and their labels to recognize patterns and features that distinguish different breeds. It figures out what makes a poodle a poodle or a bulldog a bulldog. This is machine learning! Once the model has been trained on enough labeled data, we test it out. We give the computer new dog photos it's never seen before and ask it to identify the breeds. If it classifies most of the new photos correctly, the model is working well! If not, we tweak the algorithm and training data until the computer gets better at recognizing dog breeds.

The cool thing is, the computer learns to recognize dogs all by itself, just by looking at tons of examples. Unlike normal computer programs, we don't have to code explicit rules like "IF fluffy AND curly tail THEN poodle." The machine learning model figures out the patterns on its own through exposure to data. With some help, the machine (computer) has figured out a way to learn by itself. Thus, machine learning takes data, labels it, runs algorithms to find patterns, and keeps improving its accuracy through testing. This lets computers teach themselves tasks like image recognition, language translation and even driving cars - no complicated programming required!

Machine Learning Methods

There are a few main types of machine learning models that allow computers to learn. The easiest one to understand is called supervised learning, one with which you are somewhat familiar based on a previous example. In supervised learning, we give the computer a ton of examples that are labeled with the right answer. For instance, we could feed it a dataset of photos of dogs. Each photo is labeled with the breed of dog in it - "beagle," "poodle," "bulldog," and so on. Using this labeled data, the computer can learn over time to recognize different dog breeds by detecting patterns in the photos. When it sees floppy ears, short legs, and a compact body, it learns "Aha! This must be a dachshund!" That's supervised learning in a nutshell.

Another method is unsupervised learning. Here, the computer isn't given labeled data upfront. It's given a big dataset, like a mix of dog photos, and has to find patterns and groupings on its own. The computer detects that beagles often have long, droopy ears and golden retrievers often have thick fur, without being told the breed names initially.

Finally, there is reinforcement learning. This is like rewarding the computer when it gets something right, like training a dog with treats. The more the number of right answers, the more it reinforces the correct behavior. Self-driving cars use this technique as they learn driving skills through practice. While those other methods are cool, supervised learning is the easiest to grasp. It's like teaching a kid - you provide lots of labeled examples upfront, and they gradually learn from those examples. Show enough photos of corgis and bulldogs, and the computer will learn to tell them apart.

Supervised learning requires two key ingredients: labeled data, and a machine learning algorithm. Together, these enable the computer to take the examples and gradually learn the patterns to make correct predictions on its own. That's the amazing power of machine learning!

Applying ML

Machine learning is used in all sorts of ways today. Some common uses are image recognition, language translation, chatbots, product recommendations, and self-driving cars. The possibilities are really exciting!

However, machine learning also has its limitations. The technology today is still fairly narrow in what it can do. A computer can get incredibly good at specific tasks like playing chess or identifying tumors in medical scans. But general intelligence like humans have? Not so much. It is important to remember these are human-built tools. Machine learning needs huge amounts of data that people label and input to train the models. The algorithms were created by programmers and data scientists. So while the results can seem magical, AI only works thanks to human effort.

There are also ethical concerns to keep in mind. Machine learning could perpetuate biases if the training data contains imbalances. And AI should not be used to unfairly surveil or control people. As this technology grows more powerful, we have to ensure it's applied responsibly.

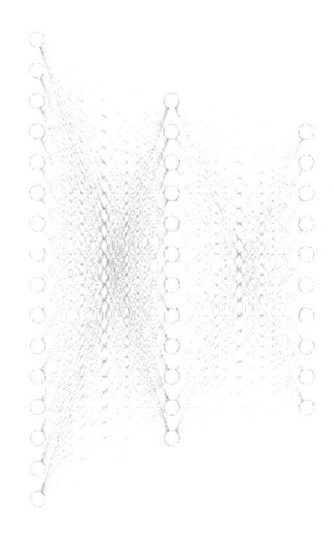

Deep Learning

Next, we consider deep learning. Deep learning is a more advanced subfield of machine learning that uses neural networks to achieve state-of-the-art accuracy on complex tasks like image recognition, natural language processing and playing games like chess or Go. Let us look at how deep learning works.

The Basics of Deep Learning

Deep learning is a fascinating field of artificial intelligence that tries to imitate the amazing power of the human brain. One key element of deep learning is that it uses neural networks, which are layers of simple computing nodes modeled after the neurons in our brains. The neurons in our brains are all interconnected and work together to understand the world around us. Similarly, the artificial neurons in a neural network are connected and signal each other, just like biological neurons do.

Fig. A Deep Learning Network

These neural connections have numeric weights that make the signals stronger or weaker as they flow between the nodes. The weights get tuned and updated as the network is trained on lots of example data, like photos, text documents, or audio clips. The neural network continually compares its predictions on the training data to the actual labels, and adjusts the connection weights in order to get the predictions right. Over time, by repeating this process, the network learns to recognize patterns all on its own!

For example, you could train a neural network to recognize cat photos by showing it thousands and thousands of images of cats, gradually tweaking the connection weights until it gets accurate at telling a cat apart from a dog or a bird. The exciting thing is that deep learning allows computers to learn straight from huge sets of data, like how we learn best from lots of real-world experience. No need to code rigid rules - neural networks figure things out based on patterns in data, just like our noggins do!

Deep learning thus uses brain-inspired neural networks that train themselves by analyzing lots of examples. This gives computers some of the amazing learning capabilities that come naturally to humans. The more data they get, the smarter the networks become!

Training a Neural Network

So how do these brain-mimicking neural networks actually learn? Let's walk through the training process step-by-step. First, we start by feeding the network a ton of labeled training data. This can be images, text, audio clips, or anything with distinct patterns. The data gets labeled so the network knows the "right answer." For example, we might give it a data set of dog photos where each photo is labeled as a certain breed, like "beagle," "poodle," or "bulldog." This helps the network learn the unique features of each breed.

Next, the network makes predictions about the training data. It identifies patterns in each dog photo and guesses the breed. Of course, at the start, the guesses will probably be wildly wrong! But here's where the learning kicks in. The network compares its guesses to the actual labels and calculates how far off it is. This gives it a numeric error score. Then the neural network goes back and slightly tweaks the connection weights between neurons to reduce the errors. It's still guessing, but thanks to the weight changes, the guesses get a bit more accurate each time.

When the same dog photos are run through again, the network gets a little better at identifying the breeds correctly. By repeating this thousands of times, the network keeps improving its accuracy. Over time, by analyzing tons of correctly labeled data, the neural network learns to recognize really complex patterns, like the visual differences between dog breeds, often better than humans can!

It's like the network gets trained through practice, just like we do. With enough repetition and weight adjustments, neural networks can master all sorts of cool skills. The more data they train on, the more accurate they become!

The future of machine learning and deep learning are bright indeed, but they also raise serious questions. How will they impact jobs? Should we regulate AI development? Can we make sure that they benefit all people equally? These are some questions we will consider in a future chapter.

Chapter 5

From the Mouths of Experts

Artificial intelligence is shaping the future, but it didn't happen overnight. Over the years, the development of AI has benefited from the genius of many people. We will hear from some of the top innovators who helped shape AI in this chapter. Prominent individuals from a range of businesses have different viewpoints on the possible implications and difficulties of artificial intelligence (AI), a topic that is fast growing. While this list is not exhaustive, it is always important to identify and understand the viewpoints of key people in any domain. Here is a more detailed look at their opinions:

Sam Altman, OpenAI's CEO

Sam Altman is a well-known name in the AI field, and he has a very upbeat outlook on how AI could change the world. According to Altman, AI has the potential to outperform even the revolutionary effects of early breakthroughs like electricity and fire. He imagines a time when AI will be used as a potent weapon against serious global problems like sickness and poverty. In Altman's opinion, the proper use of AI may change industries, boost productivity, and enhance people's quality of life all across the world.

Altman does acknowledge that there are considerable hazards associated with such enormous potential. He is fully cognizant of the potential ethical, social, and economic difficulties that AI may present. Altman highlights the significance of ensuring that the advantages of AI are available to everyone, regardless of socioeconomic class or geographic location, as AI develops. In order to prevent escalating already existing inequities, he supports regulations that encourage a just and equitable sharing of AI's benefits.

Elon Musk, Founder of Tesla

Elon Musk has a long connection with AI, and he was in fact one of OpenAI's co-founders, but later dropped out of the company, long before it released ChatGPT. Elon's views suggest that he approaches AI with more caution. He acknowledges that AI has the potential to improve a variety of industries, but he is also gravely concerned about the risks that could arise from unrestrained AI research. He has even compared AI to nuclear weapons in an effort to warn that, if not properly governed, it could endanger humanity.

The lack of regulatory control in AI research is Musk's main worry. He thinks that in the absence of appropriate rules and regulations, AI systems might be used without sufficient safety precautions, which could have unforeseen repercussions. Musk is a supporter of strict governance and ethical frameworks that put safety and human values first in order to ensure that AI is developed ethically. In order to ensure that AI research and application are carried out with the highest caution and responsibility, he argues for the creation of institutions and policies.

Musk recently announced the creation of a new company called X AI devoted to responsibly advancing artificial intelligence. The company will focus on creating transparent AI systems that can articulate their decision-making processes in a way humans can understand. Musk said X AI will allow AI developers "to see how the AI thinks and why it makes certain decisions." He hopes X AI will set a new gold standard for ethical, thoughtful AI design that other companies will follow, leading to AI that truly augments human abilities. Given Musk's profile, X AI is sure to quickly become an influential player in the high-stakes world of AI safety research.

Yoshua Bengio, Deep Learning Pioneer

Deep learning pioneer Yoshua Bengio provides insight into the state of AI today and its limits. He calls AI "narrow and brittle," emphasizing how most AI systems do well at performing narrowly defined tasks but fall short when it comes to generalizing knowledge and responding to novel circumstances.

Artificial general intelligence (AGI), which refers to AI systems with the capacity to reason and comprehend the world at a level equivalent to human intelligence, is a goal strongly supported by Bengio. He thinks that in order to attain AGI, it is crucial to learn more about how the human brain works and how neural networks and biological processes contribute to intelligence.

Bengio believes that cognitive and neuroscience research is essential for directing the creation of AI systems that can learn, generalize, and adapt just like people. In order to create more adaptable and flexible AI systems, he promotes multidisciplinary collaborations between specialists in AI and other scientific domains.

"The Godfather of deep learning" Geoffrey Hinton

One of the pioneers of deep learning, Geoffrey Hinton is internationally recognized for his contributions to the development of AI. Hinton's viewpoint focuses on the necessity of updating AI datasets and algorithms to produce more intelligent machines.

He berates modern AI models for not having a thorough comprehension of reality. Although AI has made great progress in a number of specific tasks, Hinton contends that these systems frequently lack the reasoning and knowledge generalization skills necessary for attaining real intelligence. He urges the use of fresh methods in AI research that could help us comprehend the fundamentals of human intelligence better.

Hinton imagines a time where AI helpers can relate to people as dependable friends and have empathy for them. He thinks that for AI to succeed, it must advance beyond simple pattern recognition and gain comprehension of context, emotions, and intentions. In Hinton's perspective, AI can be a real collaborator who can connect with people on a deeper level rather than just a tool for particular jobs.

Fei-Fei Li, Co-director of Stanford's AI Lab

Fei-Fei Li, a well-known researcher and lecturer in the field of AI, believes that AI has enormous potential to enhance human potential and improve life. She is aware of how AI can revolutionize many industries, such as healthcare, education, and environmental sustainability. AI is a useful tool for tackling complex problems and improving scientific study because of its capacity to process enormous volumes of data and spot patterns.

However, Li stresses that it is crucial that AI is developed in an ethical and responsible manner. She is an advocate for greater diversity in the AI community since it can lessen the negative biases present in the technology. To prevent sustaining societal disparities, it is essential to ensure inclusivity and justice in AI applications.

Li is a strong supporter of the viewpoint that AI should be created with an emphasis on enhancing rather than replacing human capabilities. She thinks AI systems ought to be created so they may coexist peacefully with people, boosting their skills and enabling them to make wiser judgments. AI may be used as a potent tool to address global concerns and enhance the quality of life for all people by keeping humans in the loop and prioritizing human-AI collaboration.

Andrew Ng, Google Brain Co-Founder

The well-known AI researcher and entrepreneur Andrew Ng is certain that AI has the power to fundamentally alter the healthcare industry. He views artificial intelligence as a useful tool that can help with earlier and more precise disease diagnosis, perhaps saving lives. AI can help doctors make better judgments and improve patient outcomes by analyzing massive volumes of medical data and looking for trends.

Ng warns against overestimating AI's potential, though. While AI has demonstrated tremendous accomplishments in certain jobs, it still lacks the human ability for common sense and general intelligence. Due to this constraint, AI might be excellent in specific fields yet struggle to comprehend complicated real-world situations that call for human-level comprehension and reasoning.

Demis Hassabis, DeepMind's CEO

Demis was the leader of the team that developed AlphaGO, the AI that famously defeated the GO world champion, Lee Sedol. Demis imagines a time when AI and people work in unison to solve the world's problems. He understands that AI is particularly good at digesting large volumes of data and making judgments based on that data. Humans, on the other hand, contribute special abilities like compassion, imagination, and intuition to the table. Hassabis thinks we can better tackle complicated issues if we combine the analytical strength of AI with human qualities.

Under Hassabis' direction, DeepMind has been aggressively examining how AI could help professionals in a range of industries, including healthcare and scientific research. Hassabis's idea of AI-human synergy is demonstrated through the company's partnerships with medical organizations to develop AI systems that assist in disease diagnosis and drug research.

Cynthia Breazeal, Creator of Jibo

A pioneer in the field of human-robot interaction, Cynthia Breazeal focuses on developing social robots that can comprehend and relate to people emotionally. She is adamant that in order for society to accept AI, it must be more than just a machine that performs tasks; it must exhibit human-like traits that enable sincere emotional interactions.

The goal of Breazeal is to create AI-enabled robots that can perceive and react to human emotions, allowing them to develop deep connections with their users. Such sympathetic AI can be used in a variety of industries, including healthcare, where social robots can help patients emotionally, and education, where they can effectively engage and motivate students.

Eliezer Yudkowsky, Machine Intelligence Research Institute

Eliezer Yudkowsky is a fervent supporter of AI ethics and safety. He issues a warning regarding the dangers that could arise from the creation of complex AI systems. A lack of appropriate prudence and ethical standards could have unforeseen repercussions or even threaten humanity's existence.

To ensure that AI systems behave ethically, Yudkowsky highlights the significance of matching AI's objectives with human ideals. Yudkowsky thinks we can prevent situations in which AI can unintentionally injure people or behave against their best interests by giving safety a higher priority in AI research and development.

Ilya Sutskever, Co-Founder of OpenAI

Ilya Sutskever is one of the co-founders of OpenAI. He asserts that artificial intelligence (AI) may overtake human intelligence within a few decades. One of humanity's biggest concerns may be how to transition to digital superintelligences.

Sutskever underlines the significance of incorporating human values into the design of new AI systems. As AI develops into superintelligence, it is essential to make sure that these potent agents act in accordance with human interests and prevent any unanticipated negative outcomes.

Satya Nadella, CEO of Microsoft

In order to avoid relying on "black box" solutions, Satya Nadella urges businesses to embrace AI as a core skill. Satya Nadella is adamant that AI will change every industry. In the future, he sees AI influencing many facets of corporate operations, from boosting productivity to tailoring customer experiences.

Nadella is dedicated to democratizing AI so that it is available to people and organizations of all sizes. He sees a world where AI platforms and tools are accessible to everyone and are easy to use, allowing more people to use AI to solve issues and spur creativity.

Yann LeCun, Facebook AI Research

Yann LeCun Leading expert in AI Yann LeCun is a proponent of AI systems that enhance and supplement human abilities. LeCun contends that creativity and common sense, which present AI systems lack, are essential components of intelligence.

LeCun advises concentrating on creating AI systems that can collaborate with people in a positive way in order to produce AI that can actually improve human intelligence. In order to provide AI systems the ability to learn more independently and comprehend complicated real-world settings better, research is being done in areas like reinforcement learning and unsupervised learning. LeCun sees a time when artificial intelligence (AI) bridges the gap between human and machine intelligence, enhancing human capabilities and assisting in the solution of humanity's most pressing problems.

Mo Gawdat, Former Chief Business Officer, Google X

Mo Gawdat, also the author of a popular book, Solve for Happy, has an optimistic yet cautious perspective on artificial intelligence. He believes AI has immense potential to automate jobs and tasks, freeing up human creativity and time for higher pursuits. However, Gawdat also recognizes the risks of superintelligent systems and the need to align advanced AI with human values and ethics. He advocates for policies to smooth the transition and distribute the benefits, along with designing AI thoughtfully with emotional intelligence and compassion in mind. Overall, Gawdat argues we can harness the power of AI to improve lives if we steward it carefully and humanistically, creating wise governance and democratizing access to shape an ethical, benevolent AI that enhances human potential while mitigating the existential risks.

Chapter 6

Applications of AI

In this Chapter, we will consider three simple application areas where AI has a significant impact: at home, in healthcare, and in environmental protection and sustainability. We will look at each category in more detail. Obviously, AI has a lot more applications than the ones listed here, but these should give you a good idea of its amazing potential.

AI at Home

Imagine having your own personal robot assistant at home! While we don't have Rosie the robot maid from The Jetsons yet, artificial intelligence is becoming a bigger part of our home lives every day. Let us explore some of the ways AI is making people's homes smarter and their lives a little easier.

Intelligent Virtual Assistants

One of the most common ways people interact with AI at home is through virtual assistants like Alexa, Siri, and Google Assistant. These systems use natural language processing to understand what you say and respond in a human-like way. You can ask them questions, have them set alarms or timers, play music, and control smart home devices. For example, you might say "Alexa, set an alarm for 8AM" so that you can wake up in time for school. Or you can ask Google Assistant "what's the weather forecast today?" to help plan your day. Virtual assistants just keep getting smarter over time as they process more data. It is inevitable that AI gets more integrated into these assistants to make our lives easier.

Smart Appliances

From refrigerators to washing machines, more and more home appliances are gaining AI-powered features to make them smarter and more convenient. For example, a smart fridge can scan what's inside and remind you when you're running low on milk or eggs. Some fridges can even provide cooking assistance by searching for recipes based on what's in your fridge!

Smart ovens have built-in cameras to photograph the food inside, allowing an app to monitor cooking progress and adjust temperature or time automatically. The app can tell you when your dish is ready without having to open the oven door.

Smart washing machines and dryers can sense how much laundry is inside and automatically select the right wash cycle. They can also alert you on your phone when the load is done. Who doesn't want to avoid that moldy forgotten laundry smell?

Home Security

AI is playing a growing role in home security systems and cameras. Smart security systems can detect suspicious activity and distinguish between a real threat and a false alarm better than older systems. Smart cameras equipped with computer vision can recognize people, animals, and objects. If someone is detected on your property when you're not home, you can get a smartphone alert. The cameras can even tell the difference between a stranger and a family member. No more annoying false alarms! The AI in home security systems is always learning and improving over time. The more data the systems collect, the better they become at recognizing potential threats and alerting homeowners.

The Future of AI at Home

AI has already made the leap from sci-fi to the real world of our homes. As the technology keeps evolving, artificially intelligent systems will become even more integrated into our daily domestic lives. Soon, smart homes that anticipate and serve our needs may not seem so futuristic after all!

AI in Healthcare

Another area where AI has made significant strides is in the important field of healthcare. AI-powered systems and algorithms are revolutionizing medical diagnostics, drug discovery, and personalized medicine. For example, AI algorithms can analyze medical images, such as X-rays and MRI scans, to assist doctors in detecting diseases like cancer at an early stage. This technology has the potential to improve diagnostic accuracy and save lives.

Medical Imaging and Diagnostics

One of the significant contributions of AI in healthcare is in medical imaging and diagnostics. AI algorithms can analyze medical images, such as X-rays, MRIs, and CT scans, to assist in the detection and diagnosis of various conditions and diseases. These algorithms excel in pattern recognition, allowing for more accurate and efficient interpretation of medical images. AI-powered diagnostic systems can detect abnormalities, lesions, or early signs of diseases, assisting radiologists and physicians in making informed decisions. For example, AI algorithms have demonstrated remarkable accuracy in detecting breast cancer, lung cancer, and other types of cancer from medical imaging, potentially enabling earlier detection and improving patient outcomes.

Furthermore, AI algorithms can analyze large datasets of medical images, patient records, and genetic information to identify patterns and correlations that may not be easily discernible to human observers. This data-driven approach can aid in the discovery of new biomarkers, the identification of disease risk factors, and the development of personalized treatment plans.

Transforming the Lives of Doctors and Patients

AI is changing how doctors treat patients. AI systems can scan a patient's health data and symptoms then give recommendations to help doctors make faster, more accurate choices about care. This can spot dangerous drug combos, suggest treatment plans, and even predict how a patient will do.

AI virtual assistants are also being used to help patients directly. These robot helpers can answer patient questions, remind them about meds, give health tips, and monitor them remotely. The AI uses language processing and deep learning to understand and respond to patients. Wearables and remote monitoring powered by AI are big too. They collect real-time data like heart rate and activity levels. AI studies the data to see patterns and give doctors early warnings if something seems off. This allows doctors to catch issues early and be proactive.

But there are ethical concerns as AI spreads in healthcare. Patient privacy, data security, and avoiding bias in the AI are crucial issues. Doctors still need to oversee AI and make the final calls on care. AI should assist human providers, not replace them. Overall, it is clear that AI has tons of potential to improve healthcare if implemented responsibly! It can complement doctors with data-driven insights and support patients with personalized care.

Drug Discovery and Development

AI is also driving advancements in drug discovery and development. With its ability to process and analyze vast amounts of biological and chemical data, AI can help identify potential drug candidates, predict their efficacy, and optimize their molecular structures. This accelerates the drug discovery process, leading to faster development of new treatments for various diseases. AI has the potential to streamline and accelerate this process, saving time and resources.

Personalized Medicine

AI is making a huge impact in personalized medicine, which is all about customizing treatment for each patient. By scanning a patient's genetic data and health records, AI can spot patterns and links to help tailor therapies. This means more effective treatments that target the problem and avoid bad reactions. For example, with cancer patients, AI looks at their genetic profile to ID specific mutations. Then it can recommend precision therapies like targeted drugs or immunotherapies that hit those mutations.

Instead of one-size-fits-all treatment, personalized medicine uses the power of AI data analysis to match the therapy to the individual. This improves chances of success and reduces risky side effects. AI is thus enabling doctors to provide super customized care by finding patterns in complex data. The future is all about targeted therapies fine-tuned for each person's unique biology!

Environmental Protection and Sustainability

AI algorithms can analyze massive amounts of climate data, like temperature records, greenhouse gas levels, and satellite images, to model the Earth's climate. This climate modeling creates detailed projections to help scientists and leaders understand climate change and make plans to address it. AI climate analysis provides more accurate future forecasts to guide smarter strategies against global warming. Let us take a look at some ways AI can help us protect the environment and make progress towards sustainability.

AI for Smarter Energy

AI is huge for optimizing energy use and improving efficiency. Smart power grids use AI to balance energy supply and demand in real-time, reducing waste. AI studies energy patterns to enhance generation from renewable sources and storage. It can also optimize where to place solar panels and wind turbines to maximize green power. For transportation, AI manages traffic flow, reduces congestion, and improves fuel efficiency to cut emissions. Self-driving cars use AI to take optimal routes and enhance sustainability.

AI for Resource Management

AI helps optimize natural resource use. It analyzes data on availability, usage, and environmental impact to sustainably manage essentials like water and materials. For water, AI irrigation systems deliver precise amounts based on crop needs, weather, and soil. This cuts waste and improves farming. For waste management, AI identifies recyclables to enhance recycling and plans optimal collection routes to minimize fuel use.

AI for Conservation

AI analyzes satellite data to detect deforestation, habitat destruction, and more. This allows quick action to protect ecosystems and biodiversity. AI sensors monitor air and water pollution in real-time to identify sources and respond swiftly. Overall, AI provides valuable insights from complex data to inform environmental conservation and sustainability efforts.

Protecting Endangered Species

AI technologies are proving to be invaluable tools for protecting endangered species and delicate ecosystems. Conservation groups are deploying camera traps with integrated AI analytics to identify and monitor wildlife populations. The AI algorithms can rapidly process thousands of images from remote locations and accurately identify animal species, allowing conservationists to study migration patterns, habitat usage, and population sizes. Drones equipped with AI cameras can survey larger territories to detect poaching activities, illegal deforestation, and other threats to wildlife. The insights gained from AI-enabled systems allow conservationists to precisely target their interventions and develop data-driven strategies to safeguard biodiversity. Initiatives like Microsoft's AI for Earth grant AI computing power to environmental projects, including an AI system that listens to bird calls to track avian populations. With the wealth of data AI systems can rapidly analyze, conservation efforts can be expanded and enhanced to preserve precious wildlife.

Despite all these applications, we should remember that AI is not a silver bullet solution. Thoughtful integration and oversight are critical to ensure AI sustainability initiatives are transparent, ethical, and socially equitable. When developed responsibly and for the benefit of both humanity and the planet, AI has immense potential to empower environmental stewardship, conserve biodiversity, curb pollution and emissions, and accelerate the transition to a sustainable world.

Chapter 7

Ethical Considerations in AI

Artificial intelligence promises to make our lives easier and more efficient in many ways. But developing thinking machines also raises important ethical questions. How can we make sure AI remains safe, unbiased, and aligned with human values? In this chapter, we'll explore some of the ethical issues surrounding AI.

AI Bias

One major concern with AI systems is the fact that they could falsely discriminate among users or consumers due to existing problems in the data. This is also referred to as 'algorithmic bias'. Since AI learns from data, any biases in that training data get incorporated into the system. This can lead to problems like facial recognition that works better for certain ethnicities over others. Or you could have resume screening algorithms that reject qualified applicants who are physically handicapped or are women, for example. These examples show why diversity in AI development is important. Teams that are homogeneous are more likely to overlook biases in training data. If team members are well represented and diverse, it is more likely that the data used to train the AI model will be fair and just. Getting input from underrepresented groups can also help identify potential fairness issues early in the design process.

Transparency

Another key value for ethical AI is transparency. When an AI system makes an important decision, like approving someone for a loan, the reasoning behind it should be explainable. Otherwise, it's difficult to appeal or fix mistakes. But with neural networks and deep learning, even designers struggle to explain internally how AIs arrive at conclusions. More transparency is needed, but it's a challenge with complex AI models. Until solved, governments may need to regulate use of "black box" AIs for certain high-stakes decisions impacting people's lives. Also, it will be important to have a human in the loop before making a final decision.

Job Loss

AI will transform the job market, replacing many routine and predictable jobs. But it may also create new job categories we can't yet imagine. The key ethical question is how to distribute AI's economic benefits broadly so fewer are left behind. Solutions could include job training, universal basic income, or payroll taxes funding communities impacted by automation.

One of the biggest worries about AI is that it could take away a lot of jobs from people. A recent study by Oxford University found that up to 47% of US jobs are at high risk of being replaced by robots and AI in the next 10-20 years. That's almost half! Jobs like truck driving, office work, and food service are likely to be automated or semi-automated, meaning that fewer humans would be required to do the heavy lifting. Losing your job to a robot could really disrupt people's lives. Without a steady job, it's hard to pay your bills and take care of your family. That's why ethicists say we really need to think about how to distribute AI's economic benefits broadly, so fewer people end up jobless and struggling.

One idea that's gaining support is the concept of a universal basic income (UBI). This means the government would give every citizen a set amount of money each month to cover basic needs, regardless of whether they have a job or not. For example, Finland ran an experiment giving people 560 euros per month and found it increased happiness while not reducing work incentives. UBI could provide a cushion for those who lose jobs to AI automation. Retraining programs for new AI-related jobs is another option. Or taxes on companies benefitting from AI could fund communities impacted by automation.

The bottom line is AI will bring huge changes to the job market. With thoughtful policies, we can share the prosperity created by these amazing new technologies. Young people like you will inherit this AI-powered world, so start thinking now about how to make it fair for all!

AI Safety

Advanced AI could become very powerful and harmful if programmed incorrectly. That's why many experts say it's crucial AI be created to align with human values and interests. This is a hugely complex technical challenge requiring extensive research and testing before deployment.

No easy answers exist for these issues. But by considering ethics early in AI education and development, we can maximize this technology's benefits while minimizing harm. The more diverse voices engaged in discussions, the better our chances of getting it right. AI will shape the future—so we must guide it thoughtfully.

As Artificial Intelligence (AI) continues to advance and permeate various aspects of our lives, it is essential to address the ethical considerations that arise with its development and deployment.

In the next chapter, we'll explore the future of AI and its potential impact on various domains, from education to governance. Join us as we dive into the possibilities and challenges that lie ahead in the era of artificial intelligence.

Chapter 8

The Future of AI

As we look ahead, the future of Artificial Intelligence (AI) holds immense possibilities and potential for transformative advancements across various domains. In this chapter, we'll explore some of the exciting prospects of AI and the challenges that lie ahead as we navigate this rapidly evolving landscape.

As we have already discussed, one of the promising areas for the future of AI is in healthcare. AI has already made significant contributions to medical diagnostics, personalized medicine, and patient care. However, the future holds even greater possibilities. AI algorithms can continue to improve diagnostic accuracy, leading to earlier detection and more effective treatment of diseases. The integration of AI with wearable devices and remote monitoring technologies can enable continuous health monitoring, providing personalized insights and proactive interventions.

Similarly, AI-powered robots and automation systems are expected to play a more significant role in industries and everyday life. From autonomous vehicles to robotic assistants, the integration of AI with robotics can enhance efficiency, productivity, and safety in various sectors. These advancements can revolutionize transportation, manufacturing, agriculture, and even household tasks, improving quality of life and freeing humans from mundane and repetitive work.

Education is another domain that stands to benefit from AI advancements. Personalized learning experiences, adaptive tutoring systems, and AI-powered virtual assistants can transform education, catering to individual learning styles and needs. AI algorithms can analyze vast amounts of educational data, identify learning patterns, and provide personalized recommendations and interventions to enhance student outcomes.

AI is also expected to have a significant impact on the field of creativity and entertainment. AI algorithms are already capable of generating music, art, and literature, blurring the lines between human and machine creativity. In the future, AI could become collaborative partners with humans in creative endeavors, assisting in the ideation, design, and production processes. This fusion of human creativity and AI capabilities can lead to groundbreaking innovations in art, music, and storytelling.

In the realm of governance and public services, AI has the potential to drive more efficient and inclusive decision-making processes. AI algorithms can analyze vast amounts of data, identify patterns, and provide insights to inform policy development and resource allocation. Additionally, AI can facilitate citizen engagement through chatbots, virtual assistants, and predictive analytics, enabling governments to better understand and address the needs of their constituents.

However, along with the possibilities, the future of AI also presents significant challenges that need to be addressed. One of the foremost concerns is the ethical and responsible development of AI. As AI systems become more autonomous and capable, ensuring that they align with human values, respect privacy, avoid biases, and prioritize safety and accountability becomes paramount. Ethical guidelines, regulations, and ongoing dialogue among stakeholders are essential to address these challenges and ensure that AI benefits all of society.

Another challenge to consider is the potential impact of AI on employment and the workforce. As automation technologies advance, there is a concern about job displacement and the need for reskilling and upskilling to adapt to the changing job market. The future will require proactive measures to ensure a just transition, providing opportunities for skill development and supporting individuals in navigating the evolving nature of work in an AI-driven world.

The responsible use of AI in decision-making is also a critical challenge. As AI algorithms influence various aspects of our lives, transparency, accountability, and the avoidance of discriminatory outcomes are of utmost importance. It is crucial to establish mechanisms for explaining AI decisions, detecting and addressing biases, and ensuring that human oversight is maintained in critical decision-making processes.

Data privacy and security will continue to be crucial concerns in the future of AI. As AI systems rely on vast amounts of data, it is essential to safeguard personal information, protect against data breaches, and ensure that individuals have control over their data. Striking a balance between data access for AI development and privacy protection will require robust regulations and technological advancements in data protection mechanisms.

Interdisciplinary collaboration and ongoing research will be key to addressing these challenges and unlocking the full potential of AI. Collaboration among AI experts, ethicists, policymakers, social scientists, and representatives from various sectors will foster a comprehensive understanding of the implications of AI and guide responsible development and deployment.

Furthermore, public engagement and education about AI are crucial for ensuring informed decision-making and promoting a broader understanding of its benefits and limitations. It is essential to involve diverse perspectives and address concerns and questions from the public to build trust, address biases, and promote inclusivity in the development and deployment of AI systems.

The technical progress with AI is not stopping anytime soon. One of the most exciting possibilities on the horizon is the possible realization of AGI or Artificial General Intelligence. Let us look more closely at the implications of this development.

Towards AGI and Superintelligence

Smarter than Humans

Imagine a sort of AI that is as smart and capable as the human brain. "Artificial general intelligence" or AGI is another name for this sophisticated AI. "Superintelligence" refers to AI that is even more superior to human intelligence and goes beyond AGI. Some scientists think that when we get to superintelligence, we could have machines that may be up to a billion times smarter than humans within a few decades. That is like comparing the human brain to an ant brain. Now imagine that we humans were in the position of the ants. That type of capability would be so powerful that it would literally alter the course of humanity. The question is whether it can understand human values and act in ways that help us do better.

In the early stages, AGI may look like a robot with general human-level intelligence. It might be able to comprehend language, pick up new abilities, work out riddles, form plans, and be creative. Similar to how people learn, it might educate itself by reading books and watching films. Some people are rightly concerned that if AGI is developed, it may grow to be far smarter than humans and challenging to control.

AGI, though, has a ton of interesting potential advantages. AGI may come up with solutions to large-scale issues like disease and climate change. Or help us as virtual assistants that are far more intelligent than Siri or Alexa. Strong AGI will require extensive research and careful consideration to ensure that it is both safe and advantageous for humanity.

How to Create AGI

Scientists must discover a way to create machines that can comprehend and think like people if they are to develop an AI that is as intelligent as humans. This is very challenging! Even seemingly straightforward tasks that come naturally to humans, like object recognition or communication, are quite challenging for AIs to master.

Our most advanced AIs can currently only excel at specific tasks like playing chess or Go, or recognizing faces. Researchers think AIs must master critical skills including reasoning, problem-solving, language, and common sense in order to reach human intelligence. Some experts believe that all we need to accomplish this is bigger and faster AIs. Others think we require entirely new AI methodologies and structures. There is much discussion on whether current AI techniques are sufficient to eventually achieve AGI on par with humans or whether fundamentally new methods are required.

The brain is a very complicated organ! It will take significant scientific advances to replicate all of its powers in machines. The exact date that AGI or superintelligence will appear is unknown. If advancements continue, many experts believe it could occur within the next few decades. But there are significant obstacles to overcome. There is little doubt that a lot more research and development will be required to create AI that is smarter than humans.

The Dawn of a New Era

Artificial general intelligence (AGI), or AI that is generally as smart as humans, would be a big concern and lead to significant social upheaval. The possibility of widespread employment automation is a significant implication. Robots with AGI would be capable of carrying out numerous jobs now done by people. Many human workers could be replaced by this. AGI may potentially lead to the emergence of new sectors and jobs that we haven't even begun to envision. However, if workers aren't ready with the most recent abilities, the shift could be difficult.

Making sure AGI is in line with human values and objectives is another crucial challenge. A harmful super-advanced AI could result from improper design. Because of this, many experts believe that new laws and policies regarding the development of AGI are necessary. Technology must be developed responsibly and with consideration for its effects on society.

If the algorithms are educated on faulty data reflecting societal prejudices, there are also worries that AGI could worsen already-existing biases and inequities. Fairness and transparency in AI systems are being worked on.

In the future, it's conceivable that AGI and limited AI will collaborate to enhance human capabilities. It will be crucial to strike the correct balance. AGI, if carefully created and applied, could contribute to humanity's flourishing by supporting us in overcoming significant obstacles. But we must make plans in advance and responsibly manage its development. There are exciting times ahead!

In conclusion, the future of AI, and eventually AGI, holds immense promise and potential across multiple domains, including healthcare, education, creativity, governance, and beyond. However, to fully realize these possibilities, it is crucial to navigate the challenges associated with ethics, employment, decision-making, and data privacy. By fostering responsible development, ensuring inclusivity, and engaging in ongoing dialogue, we can shape a future where AI is a powerful tool for positive transformation and benefits humanity as a whole.

Chapter 9

Resources for your AI Journey

By now, I hope you are convinced about the importance of AI in your future. There are many amazing resources out there that you can start exploring as you learn and practice your new AI skills. The goal of this chapter is to provide you enough information so that you can start your journey today. Please check out the URLs for these resources, and spend some time familiarizing yourself with what is being offered. You don't need to be a programmer or a computer expert to start learning right away.

Online Courses and Tutorials

Codecademy

- What it offers: Interactive courses on Python, JavaScript, and Data Science.

- Why it's important: Python is one of the most widely used languages in AI. Learning it will give you a head start.
- Level: Beginner to Intermediate

Coursera

- What it offers: Courses from top universities like Stanford and MIT on AI, machine learning, and data science.
- Why it's important: Provides a deep understanding of AI from academic leaders in the field.
- Level: Beginner to Advanced

Udacity

- What it offers: Specialized "Nanodegree" programs in AI, machine learning, and robotics.
- Why it's important: These are industry-aligned courses designed to make you job-ready.
- Level: Intermediate to Advanced

Coursera

- What it offers: Coursera provides a wide range of courses from accredited universities and institutions around the world. Topics cover everything from basic Python programming to specialized AI and machine learning courses.
- Why it's important: The platform offers a blend of theoretical and practical knowledge, often with peer-reviewed assignments and certificates upon completion. This makes it a valuable resource for both learning and career advancement.
- Level: Beginner to Advanced

MIT OpenCourseWare

- What it offers: MIT OpenCourseWare (OCW) offers free course materials for a wide range of MIT courses, including video lectures, assignments, and exams. The courses in AI and machine learning are particularly strong.
- Why it's important: MIT is a leading institution in technology and engineering. The open courseware allows you to access

high-quality educational materials for free, providing a self-paced but rigorous learning experience.
- Level: Intermediate to Advanced

YouTube Channels and Podcasts

MrEflow

- What it offers: Tutorials and explanations on machine learning, data science, and AI.
- Why it's important: The channel breaks down complex topics into easy-to-understand videos, making it great for beginners.
- Level: Beginner to Intermediate

AI Explained Official

- What it offers: The channel focuses on explaining AI concepts, technologies, and their applications in layman's terms.
- Why it's important: It demystifies AI, making it accessible to a general audience, including those without a technical background.
- Level: Beginner

3Blue1Brown

- What it offers: Visual explanations of complex mathematical concepts.
- Why it's important: Math is the backbone of AI, and this channel makes it accessible.
- Level: Beginner to Advanced

Lex Fridman Podcast

- What it offers: In-depth interviews with leading AI researchers.
- Why it's important: Provides insights into the cutting-edge developments in AI.
- Level: Intermediate to Advanced

Websites and Blogs

Towards Data Science

- What it offers: Articles, tutorials, and news on AI, machine learning, and data science.
- Why it's important: Keeps you updated with the latest trends and technologies.

OpenAI Blog

- What it offers: Research papers, articles, and updates on OpenAI projects.
- Why it's important: OpenAI is at the forefront of AI research.

Software and Tools

Google Colab

- What it offers: A cloud-based Python notebook with free GPU support.
- Why it's important: Allows you to run heavy AI models without a powerful computer.

Jupyter Notebooks

- What it offers: An open-source web application for live code and data visualization.
- Why it's important: Widely used for data analysis and machine learning.

TensorFlow Playground

- What it offers: This web app allows you to experiment with TensorFlow, one of the most popular AI frameworks, using drag-and-drop blocks or code.
- Why it's important: It provides a hands-on, intuitive way to understand neural networks and machine learning algorithms.
- Level: Beginner to Intermediate

Competitions and Hackathons

Kaggle

- What it offers: Data science competitions with real-world problems.
- Why it's important: Provides hands-on experience and networking opportunities.
- Level: Beginner to Advanced

Google Code-in

- What it offers: Open source projects for pre-university students.
- Why it's important: Early exposure to real-world coding projects.
- Level: Beginner

DrivenData

- What it offers: Data science competitions focused on social impact.
- Why it's important: Allows you to apply your skills to solve meaningful problems.
- Level: Intermediate to Advanced

Topcoder

- What it offers: A platform for coding challenges, development, and design tasks.
- Why it's important: Offers cash prizes and opportunities to work on projects for big companies.
- Level: Intermediate to Advanced

Codeforces

- What it offers: Algorithmic challenges and competitive programming contests.
- Why it's important: Helps improve problem-solving skills essential for AI development.

- Level: Intermediate to Advanced

HackMIT

- What it offers: An annual hackathon hosted by MIT.
- Why it's important: Provides a platform for innovation and collaboration with like-minded individuals.
- Level: Intermediate to Advanced

AI Cyber Challenge

- What it offers: A competition focused on applying AI techniques to cybersecurity problems.
- Why it's important: It bridges the gap between AI and cybersecurity, offering a unique opportunity to apply AI skills in a critical domain.
- Level: Intermediate to Advanced

Community and Networking

Reddit AI community

- What it offers: Discussions, articles, and questions about AI.
- Why it's important: Keeps you engaged with the AI community.

LinkedIn Groups

- What it offers: Professional networking opportunities in AI.
- Why it's important: Connects you with industry professionals and potential mentors.

Consult the Table below for the full hyperlinks to all these resources.

Category	Resource	Level	Complete URL
Online Courses and Tutorials	Codecademy	Beginner to Intermediate	https://www.codecademy.com/
	Coursera	Beginner to Advanced	https://www.coursera.org/
	Udacity	Intermediate to Advanced	https://www.udacity.com/
	MIT OpenCourseWare	Intermediate to Advanced	https://ocw.mit.edu/
YouTube Channels and Podcasts	MrEflow	Beginner to Intermediate	https://www.youtube.com/user/MrEflow
	AI Explained Official	Beginner	https://www.youtube.com/@aiexplained-official
	3Blue1Brown	Beginner to Advanced	https://www.youtube.com/@3blue1brown

	Lex Fridman Podcast	Intermediate to Advanced	https://lexfridman.com/podcast/
Websites and Blogs	Towards Data Science	-	https://towardsdatascience.com/
	OpenAI Blog	-	https://www.openai.com/blog/
Software and Tools	Google Colab	-	https://colab.research.google.com/
	Jupyter Notebooks	-	https://jupyter.org/
	TensorFlow Playground	Beginner to Intermediate	https://playground.tensorflow.org/
Competitions and Hackathons	Kaggle	Beginner to Advanced	https://www.kaggle.com/
	Google Code-in	Beginner	https://codein.withgoogle.com/

	DrivenData	Intermediate to Advanced	https://www.drivendata.org/
	Topcoder	Intermediate to Advanced	https://www.topcoder.com/
	Codeforces	Intermediate to Advanced	https://codeforces.com/
	HackMIT	Intermediate to Advanced	https://hackmit.org/
	AI Cyber Challenge	Intermediate to Advanced	https://www.aicyberchallenge.com/
Community and Networking	Reddit AI community	-	https://www.reddit.com/r/artificial/
	LinkedIn Groups	-	https://www.linkedin.com/groups/

Table: List of Resources with Full URLs

A Final Word

If you made it to here, awesome job! You have just wrapped up this epic journey into the world of AI. By now, you probably get that AI is sure to change everything—school, work, art, music, the military, and pretty much everything else we can dream of! But guess what? This is just the beginning! You are the trailblazers who are going to help make AI a big part of our lives. You've got the power to change things. AI isn't just for the brainiacs; it is truly for everyone, and if you start today, you will be in the driver's seat when it comes to understanding and benefiting from future developments.

So keep digging into all the awesome stuff we have talked about—the genius creators, the key ideas, and all the cool websites and tools. Dream huge, get coding, and start making stuff! Let us aim to use AI to help people and tackle some of the world's toughest problems. The AI adventure is just getting started, and the sky's the limit! So go ahead, share your big ideas and dreams to help shape what comes next.

I truly appreciate your participation in this unique journey in this book. May your AI journey also be one of wonder, discovery, and limitless potential. If you liked this book, please help me spread the word by:

- Leaving a 5-star review on Amazon
- Telling your siblings, classmates, friends and relatives about this book
- Recommending this book to your teacher for use in class, and
- Sharing your thoughts on social media

Last but not least, do check out our other titles and stay tuned for new and exciting releases from Lexicon Labs. And if you have a younger sibling or friend, make sure they check out 'AI for Smart Kids Ages 6-9'.

I wish you lots of good luck and new adventures!

Dr. Leo Lexicon

Check out our fun, auto-themed coloring books

Hours of coloring fun for all ages!

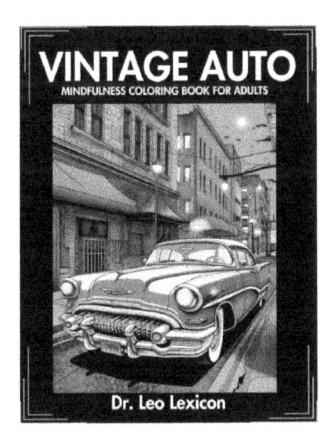

- Each book has over 40+ carefully curated HQ images
- Pefect companion for a road trip or vacation
- Try one today, you won't be disappointed
- Check out our other titles, we have all ages covered
- From the team at Lexicon Labs, bringing joy one page at a time!
- Follow Dr. Leo Lexicon on Twitter

@LeoLexicon

LEXICON LABS

LAUNCH TIME!
For Space and STEM Enthusiasts

INDIA'S MOONSHOT
HOW AMBITION, ENGINEERING, AND IMAGINATION PUT INDIA ON THE SOUTH POLE OF THE MOON
A CHAPTER BOOK FOR SMART MINDS
DR. LEO LEXICON

COMING SOON!

- Explore the Moon's South Pole: First-ever insights into uncharted lunar territory
- Inside ISRO's Success: Decades of innovation and global collaboration behind India's moon mission
- Mission Blueprint: Step-by-step guide to Chandrayaan-3's epic voyage
- STEM Inspiration: Fuel your passion for science, technology, and space
- Own a Piece of History: Relive the global celebration of a groundbreaking achievement

Follow Dr. Leo Lexicon on Twitter/X
X @LeoLexicon

LEXICON LABS

AI FOR YOUNGER READERS
Get on the leading edge of the AI revolution!

- Perfect for readers Ages 6-9
- Structured introduction to the building blocks of AI
- AI concepts explained in a simple, easy-to-understand format by a Bay Area educator
- Resources for puzzles, games, and coding
- Perfect travel companion or gift

Follow Dr. Leo Lexicon on Twitter/X

@LeoLexicon

LEXICON LABS

Discover More Bestselling Titles from Lexicon Labs!

SCAN ME